PROFOUND NONSENSE

PROFOUND NONSENSE

A Book of Poetry

Gloria Bernstein

Columbus, Ohio

Profound Nonsense: A Book of Poetry

Published by Gatekeeper Press
2167 Stringtown Rd, Suite 109
Columbus, OH 43123
www.GatekeeperPress.com

Copyright © 2018 by Gloria Bernstein

All rights reserved. Neither this book, nor any parts within it may be sold or reproduced in any form or by any electronic or mechanical means, including information storage and retrieval systems without permission in writing from the author. The only exception is by a reviewer, who may quote short excerpts in a review.

ISBN: 9781642370515

Printed in the United States of America

In Memory of:
my sister and brothers.

ACKNOWLEDGEMENTS

This book is in memory of my sister and brothers. I thank my family for their love and support, my friends for being there for me. There is a special place for my grandchildren, Hannah, Claire and Thomas, who lift my spirit and give my life a profound sense…

CONTENTS

Chapter 1: Family History: The Farm 1
Chapter 2: Senseless Things 17
             Senseless Things (Past Lives And Present) 55
Chapter 3: Family History: Growing Old 73
Chapter 4: Talking To The Prophet 103
Chapter 5: Talking To Myself:
             The Coming Of The Messiah 125
Chapter 6: Incantations: Old-Wives Tales 139
Chapter 7: Moments In Stone 147
Chapter 8: War 167
Chapter 9: Family History: The Child 185
Chapter 10: Family History: Growing Old 201

CHAPTER 1
FAMILY HISTORY: THE FARM

GOOD TIMES

The farm, tattered wretched
forlorn reeked of hay and
horses. My foot knew every rock
in stubbled fields. Nobody
remained huddled by the stove
in winter who remembered
the good times. I'm sure
there must have been some.

GOD BLESS

The horse pulled the wagon
to the porch. We moved
weary, the ride long bumpy
the boards creaked. We buried
the old man the horse too.
We knew it would happen.
That summer we picked berries.
God bless us all the horse too.

BEING TEN

At eight I knew everything.
At ten my mother died and I knew
nothing but that. Ten to twelve
are missing. At twelve I discovered
my body, but was stuck at ten.

IMPORTANT THINGS

It's important to forget pain.
Pleasure like a sickness
hangs on. Joy and passion
not words I use or recall
like summer evenings and
mosquitos. I remember where
I am but not how I got here.

MORE GOOD TIMES

Heavy rain crushed flowers
seeped into cellar flooded
dams, turned the grave
to mud. We let water drip
uncaring to the floor. Any
shelter house roof will do
out of the rain, after a burial
the mother left behind.

THAT SPRING

It rained. The green, emerald
as far as I could see, forever.
That far. My mother never
grew beyond that Spring.
Lilacs bloomed, the smell
sweet and sickening.

THEY SAID

Marriages are made in
heaven. This one in hell
forever on this God-forsaken farm.
She prayed he would cut wood
for winter, not wishing
to prolong life but if she
froze before breakfast
he'd find a way, not pleasant
to thaw her.

BEING HAPPY

They told her it would be
like this. She being plain and
stupid didn't listen. Now
getting water, the pump
thump-swished filling the pail
it was God- awful. Smarter now
even if there was time to waste
who cared about happy.

FARM LAND

The pasture rolled on, stubble
messed with cow dung bumped
into trees on its way to the sky.
The road snaked through fields
a gray house leaned on maples
the farm odorous with growing
things. Somewhere, drums and
guns echoed but not here.

THE LAST COW

My father milked, pumped
udders up and down, milk
hissed-pinged into the pail
tail swished, skin twitched
she shifted, her heat radiated
through the barn. She was sold
to pay the mortgage. Warm
milk turns my stomach.

MAKING CHEESE

My father tipped the pail
into a gauze bag, hung over
the porch railing, dripped
into the grass. A man came
for the cow, the milk curdled
to cheese the last time.

THE LAST COW

I sat on the fence, the cow gone.
Odors of damp wool sheepskin
seeped from my skin. The farm
mingled flies dung apple blossoms.
The cow persisted, ever present.

SELLING THE CALF

The cow bellowed all night
when they took her calf, said
she was a stupid animal.
She was sold. The farm died.
Every spring as sap ran in green
buds, that stupid odor mingled
with the blossoms.

THE SMELL OF HORSES

Someone smells of hay
on the supermarket line.
My heart lurches. I am back,
cow bells, my brother with
a stick jumping rocks avoiding
cow-flop, bringing the cows
home. I watch the last light
unaware of that porous odor
that clings to me.

FLIGHT

A sliver of sun cuts across
the horizon tangles in trees.
The sky is mean angry beautiful.
I long to spread my wings, fly
in a rush of leaves, far beyond
the knowing stench of farm
only for a moment, never
to leave forever.

A DISTANT LAND

Women with rings and things
chase wild pigs to the sound
of drums far from the field
where mud-spotted cows
move with bells. In the dark
of pre- morning we gather
them, as light breaks
on primitive landscapes.

THE HOUSE

In winter the house froze
to the ground unyielding. Wind
eased through walls thin as paper
windows rattled roof creaked
the heat of the stove blocked
by a wall of razor- edged cold.

TEA

The pipes froze. Mama boiled
snow to make tea. Blood, rose
red in cheeks, drained from lips
chilled lungs. We wore sweaters
to bed, ate hot soup. The snow
high, higher almost over the
house. Papa held his hands
over the stove. It didn't help.

A SLANTED MEMORY

Skeleton tools on the wall
empty stalls webbed shut.
The hunting knife, sheath rusty
with blood, jagged saw axe stuck
in stump. We climbed the wagon
drove to the brook, watered horse
past the apple orchard, stone wall.
We held tight, milk pails clanged
tumbled, we trembled, cleared
the purple juniper into the sky.

ALWAYS SOMETHING

Somebody died. She caught
a goose wrung its neck plucked
feathers gutted stuffed roasted.
Everyone came like a holiday.
Her son came home from war
with one leg. She roasted a goose
one more when the baby died.
Always one thing or another.

SOMETHING HAPPENED

The smell, roasted chicken
wafted out the door. We stopped
work, someone must've died.
Mama made a chicken couldn't
be for nothing. We washed, Papa
sat down. We waited. Nothing
happened she said, it was just
a good day. Papa sat. Maybe
he'd punch the table. He said,
you wasted a chicken for nothing.
But he just ate, forgot to punch.

KNOCK ON WOOD

Terrible things come in threes.
Beset with superstition I knock
on wood three times, watch
for the evil eye, a black bird
a sure sign. Something went
wrong. Death came even when
I knocked. I don't believe it works.

GIVING UP

I have given up believing.
I blame old age.
I am an honorable person
but can make no claims
to define this. If I had been
spiritual I would understand.
As you can see I know myself
well and it gives me no pleasure.
For that, I truly believe
I can only blame old age.

CHAPTER 2
SENSELESS THINGS

EARLY MORNING

Without a doubt the flooded brook
edged up the road as hunters
in pick-ups, dead deer tied tight
swished in muddy water over the
bridge. Even when young I sickened
now I knew it was not
a good season to die. The moon
older, also sickened,
fainted I swear, fell into the
water and drowned.

HOLDING ON

It is urgent to understand
disappointment. I struggle with
the stars, trivial things, search
for handles in the sky. The Gods
on Mt. Olympus vie for power
jealous vengeful competitive and
considering condition of the world
have a wicked sense of humor.

ANGEL

An angel with a broken wing
sat in a shaded tree turned
to face me with a twisted mouth
frightening eyes and ageless face.
All in all, profoundly human.

RHYMES

The child's tangled fingers
careful movements, secret
and repetitive longing, say it
again, over again. Fingers
unlike the mother but still
spinning the web, magic
making the sun shine for that
indomitable spider.

HORSE'S TALE

The book deceptive but passionate.
Beautiful people dancing through life
and love. Death a dark night, dragon
besetting a horse galloping, whipped
by the frantic horseman, escaping.
The ending not much better.

CONDITIONS

Pain, high on the list
things to avoid like sickness
death war. Other unpredictable
catastrophes unimagined before.
Pleasure, that human pursuit
fiercely competes, often entangled
on the same list.

ON THE EDGE

I danced on a fine line. For a minute
I believed in God.
A tree over the path, the woods
unfriendly now light slanted
the wrong way. I hesitated
in that sacred minute, the line
ended. I almost fell off the cliff.

VIRGINIA WOOLF

Three mountains away wind carried sound of honking geese over the green valley. The sun settled behind trees the moon pulled her out of bed to the lake her long white gown trembled as water inched up and the lake made room for her.

WALKING A DIRT ROAD

I could change things if
what I wanted was clear.
But I might mess up my life
everyone else's, a disaster.
It is best to leave things
to chance, hope it will be
what I wanted, didn't know
what was best until it happened
and I forgot what I started out
to want, so everything
shifted around to end up.

IT HAPPENED

yesterday late afternoon
orange sky fused hills, mountains
melted to red. I saw it, against the
four-cornered sky from the top of
a stone castle, I saw it. But never
on a quiet day in October late
afternoon did I see such a sight
or hear the eerie sound of flutes.

MIXED UP

She lived in a village, emerald
hills lavender mountains birds
and bees, yet she was an atheist.
She yearned, please if there is
a God help me. Not like Virginia
in her white gown dashed to her
destiny. A fairy fluttered fluorescent
wings said atheists go to heaven.
She doubted but a bee strayed
stung her, she shouted without
thinking, God damn it! So, she
became a believer, painfully.

THE OAK TREE

The men circled the tree
towered sixty feet in leafy
spread, symmetrical space
calculated not beauty.
Decision made it had to go.
Panicked, I held on to my soul.
Why I asked, the tree
is a hundred years old. So
he said, is my grandmother.

THE BACKYARD TREE

I went to three doctors
this week. Still I am lucky
there are no bombs falling.
The tree will be taken
down, its soul decayed
infested with ants there is
no hope. Thank God there
are no bombs, but the tree
will not survive, nor will I.

KILLING THE TREE

Like a monkey he climbed
ropes hooks to top branches
tied them swung lower
with his buzz saw, chips
sputtered. Were there screams
when limbs swung loose
on ropes and hooks, hung
free flayed, landed with a crash
a spattering of blood, maybe
cracking of bones, groaning.
The stump is left. The red
of October stark winter, shade
dismembered. Why did I watch.

ABANDONED

Wait for me I called, I'm coming.
I ran for my coat hat boots
my heavy pack, the rutted knife
in the torn pouch. Wait don't leave
without me! The gun in the closet
behind summer things, are they
waiting, some bread an apple
what did I forget, I ran out
but they were gone.
Left me alone with my gun.

THE PROPHET

When Jeremiah the prophet
ascended to heaven he was amazingly
disappointed. The state of bliss
was not exactly satisfying. No longer
having a reason to qualify his
admonitions to repent, confused
whether God cared as He was nowhere
to be found, Jeremiah expected a reward
more gratifying more soul-fulfilling.
Truthfully, he missed the people
sinful as they were who sat at his feet
listening to dire predictions. Worst of all
he wasn't sure if he had gotten it right.

ONLY IN JULY

Near the swollen brook
raspberries are ripe
on roadside bushes washed
with rain, melt in the mouth
like sugared air. I go from bush
to bush avoiding thorns, intent
on the intertwined poisonous
magentas. Large berries on a
back bush beyond a ditch
damn, out of reach!

ANOTHER KIND

A bird, its beak wide
into some kind of song
trilling high like a scream
not a song but foreboding
fear and flight, possibly
not a bird at all.

LESSONS

I am sliding on shattered glass
with bare feet. Not the first time.
Monkey sits on his tail, a spider
caught in its own web. Naked
and bloody, not the last time.
Lessons persist so hard to learn.

A DISCIPLINED THOUGHT

The man in the ad said
'I'm in love with a man a Man
called God. I'm in love with God.
Does that make me gay?' But
that question is complicated.
If I loved a tree does that make
me what? What If I was in love
with God and He was a Man
and gay. Don't get upset
it's only an ad.

CHANGES

Sometimes, I'm a wild thing
a creature startled by humans
wary, the smell of fear.
My hair grows tangled in spurs
caught in spider webs, my voice
strange but perfectly right
for the thing I've become.
I do not know what
but let it be.

WEAPONS

My nails grow long I cut them
to the skin, the look of claws
betrays me, the urge to use them
weapons sharpened to a point
for you know as well as I
how fragile life is
how frightened I've become.

WHAT IF

What if the—suddenly hits
or misses, the arrow fails
dagger slips missile strikes
can the stars fall?
But this is nonsense.
I would fix it all, everything
if I knew what to do but
what if, no I can't believe that
will happen never in a million
years. But it is a million years.

EAKINS PAINTING

Flaccid bored beauty
red dress a river from neck to toe
hands, white birds ready for flight.
I can't sit anymore. You are a monster.
Eakins was a monster, eyes wild
with immortality.

EAKINS PAINTING WHITMAN

Whitman was almost dead.
('Oh Captain! My Captain!)
White hair vaporized a crushed
face not an old man choking
on camphor, bold words on paper
('Oh, Captain! My Captain! Rise up-)
Eakins hurried his strokes Whitman
best of models sat motionless ('O Heart,
Heart! Heart!)

INTERRUPTIONS

A storm on Jupiter
wherever that is, butchered
a pig had the neighbors over.
A space ship whistled
like a bird leveled the corn
circular like. Downright criminal
to ruin a field of corn. Mars erupted
we locked up when the meteorite
landed. Didn't affect us we thought
but the cows wouldn't milk. Damn!

MY DAYS

It is a sin I know to waste my days
as though I had endless more.
My heart flips at every wrong done
the intentional destruction.
It is absurd getting even with life.

THE DESCENT OF MAN

I slid down the tree landed
on my butt. The monkey
laughed, it hurt to be grounded.
A snake rattled his tail, tempted
me down the trail of evil. The
monkey shook his head, jumped
screeched twirled his tail threw
an apple at me. I picked it up and
in my sudden wisdom knew
a major happening when it hit me.

THE ASCENT OF MAN

When I slid down the tree
landed on the ground I hardly
knew what to do. Tried it out
for centuries the ten rules
impossible, couldn't cope.
I made a mess complete failure.
There was nobody left in the tree
but I climbed back up. Haven't
ventured down since.

VISITOR

On a far mountain a castle balanced
on rock. God lived there when He
visited. We trembled with all the fire
smoke booming banging rumbling.
Weary of these intrusions I climbed
up to confront Him. The castle, dark
silent empty no sign of Him. I waited.
I called out. A mouse skittered a bat
fluttered but there was nobody and
despite the fire and smoke, surely
a prank, there never had been.

EASY TEARS

I cry a lot. When someone walks
a dog a kerchief tied on its neck
I'm a child again but
I can't remember my mother.
I look out the window at the purple
mountain I climbed slid down
on a tin sign. Once I weeded a field
of strawberries. I have lots of memories
but if someone touches me tears well up
still, I can't remember my mother.

A BAD DAY, MOSTLY WASTED

8:00 am
I don't want to get out of bed but I
have to or won't be able when I want
and hell, if I had to stay forever. I
know what that means, soiling the
sheets precisely and I'm not an
animal yet but getting

9:00 am
closer. I make the wood stove, ritual to
celebrate fire. Gather round me wolves
and jackals living in fear pretending we
enjoy life. I break the fast with oatmeal
miracle food for toothless

10:00 am
gums, absolutely. The sun comes up
intentionally, selectively wastes each
hour and like death mourns the loss
as if it were precious not an act of

1:00 pm
premeditated murder. I remember what
I threw into the fire. Time for lunch. Excited
deer glance in my window knowing I'm
hungry not desperate enough to kill yet
intuitively they hurry

2:00 pm
away. The next hour a foe, not a bull
seeing red but a mouse at night looking
for a crumb, light scaring it to a hole even
in mid-day shadows the fear of sudden

3:00 pm
sight. Now I watch the hours go by
fascinated with clouds a major event
like history and you'd never know
even if something

10:00 pm
happened like Darwin waiting
for me to develop into something
suitable for evolution even in a day
wasted as it was. Back in bed, lights
out I feel the fins growing as I slip

11:00 pm
back to the sea. Splash.

STRESS

Problems burden the day. I'd rather
dance a child on my toes than read
morning papers. The world crumbles
and the neighbor's lab is loose black
as death, it's tongue hangs over sharp
teeth, a broken chain on its neck.

KNOWING

I know why snow freezes, water stays
in the ocean but the string theory the
thirteen articles of faith are beyond me.
If after I die I return, mysteries revealed
it is likely from what I see around me
I will begin again with falling snow.

CARING

"Take care not to spoil or destroy My world,
for if you do," (Midrash)
I walk gently in the woods step over dead
trees never waste fragrance a song or
disturb a furred or winged creature. I never
carry an axe or knife, I am not a spoiler. But
last night driving home I killed a deer.

ONCE UPON A TIME

When I was someone else
and the world was perfect,
beautifully arranged, a frightening
human voice arose, turned rivers
to dust, fish lay stinking. I understood,
took up a gun knife stones, just in case.
I remember the world perfect,
I was someone else, would never
throw a stone.

HAUNTED

I recall the shrieking of birds
in the woods, an easy place to
hone skills, tightly knit trees
an arm's width in every direction
ghosts, pious thoughts nurtured
in childhood my name etched
in stone carved in green light
with a pocket knife.

SUMMER PATIO

My patio is weeded raked
swept clean, potted plants here
and there. I sit smelling pines
grass, listening to a bird sing.
My mind empty quiet, life
has shut down. Grief gone.
The phone rings.
I sit like a stone, a brick scraped
clean. The ringing stopped.
The bird sings.
I sit on my patio like any
ornamental thing.

THE AUCTION BLOCK

Tax collectors, fund raisers creditors
all want a piece of me. My doctor
fends off organ thieves hungry for
my liver, impassioned for my heart
sadists nothing less than my soul
the bounty hunter my head.
I would under circumstances
satisfy all, as they say 'an eye
for an eye' symbolically speaking
the claims now monetary. So,
how much for my heart? If I was
not dying I could be greedy.
I'd think twice about my soul,
the rates fluctuate like the stock market.
My head, five hundred years ago, stuck
on a stake by the castle gate, weighted
in gold, now not worth the unsightly damage
its loss would incur. So, friends and foes,
who first bidder and who last in line
for whatever remains.

THE PARK

Dancing on the edge of the brook
a red-winged black bird skims the
toxic fluid, the beautiful copper
color streaks the stones a poisonous
red. A heron pecks for frogs, as
the salt mixed in winter sand
leeches under the sea-saws.

THE VETERAN

He returned from war, said
he would burn the barn. In battle
he moved mountains turned
a jungle to desert. I was married
to him but he brought a refugee
woman, told me to go. I didn't
mind the woman but was afraid
of him, still at war. I left quickly
on Sunshine our horse, as the
barn burned.

THE GURU

The Guru, serene in mind
body soul, calm in meditation
of nothingness. I've tried
standing on my head blood
flowing down not struggling up
but the mind goes its own way.
I am aware of that Supreme Source
but the connection is impossible
even in an upright position.
Especially.

VALENTINE'S DAY

Love, the romantic kind ebbs
and flows. Jealousy hate passion
not steadied by candy and flowers.
I am not a Saint so unconditional
is difficult and where love
is concerned, wishful thinking.
Chocolate cherries more satisfying.
Temporarily.

THE TEN-POINTER

The deer freezes catches scent
leaps in the light as the trees
speed by. Red jacket follows
fear frenzy footsteps hoofs
crackling twigs gunshots, heavy
breathing, silence. The ten-pointer
in the gray dusk forest
has disappeared.

AMATURE HUNTER

Somewhere in the woods
a bird cries. Hunter sits on
a rock gun on lap. If a tree
moves he shoots, a flower
sways, takes careful aim
a bird flies, an easy mark
he sits gun cocked. Caught
in light between spruces a
big-eyed doe waits. The gun
goes off, misses tree, flower,
hits the deer, accidentally.

THE BROKEN DAM

White heron etched the lake
geese pecked slick slugs and
minnow, blue-backed ducks glided
over jellied frog eggs, turtles hid
fragile eggs in sand holes, birds
dipped swooped at the shimmering
surface. An ordered chaos before
the dam broke, the lake emptied
downhill taking that plentiful feast
hungry wildlife with it and in that
rush of water, a hundred years of
sunsets reflected there, vanished.

NAMING THE RIVER

The river had many names
spoken with awe respect dignity.
The Water of Swift Canoes
Many Fish, Music and Mountains
The Sparkling Drink of the Gods.
A man named Hudson sailed
down that sacred river, declared
he discovered it. I cannot grasp
the perverse nature, a man giving
a river his name. No matter,
the river remains sacred
and Henry Hudson is dead.

SENSELESS THINGS
(Past Lives and Present)

BEING THERE

No lights no sign posts
stray cats, dogs, nothing. I am lost.
If I knew where I came from
I could get back. Someone said,
'wherever you are, you are there.'
If I knew what that meant
I wouldn't be lost.

MIRACLES

A miracle happened, so simple
it almost passed unnoticed.
My mind opened, heart softened
understanding of life, clarified.
I know nothing about miracles
attribute those things to old age
which I am haplessly familiar with
however, it could have been
a miracle and like old age
I cannot say it was simple.

INSTINCTS

The moon opened tracks
into the woods. I followed.
A primitive thing furious
at being awakened, startled me,
suddenly alerted, vision sharpened
I pranced, nibbled twigs, transformed,
barely human, not animal, yet
I adjusted. Intuitively.

LISTENING

Pretended all my life
to know things, whispered or
shouted. Not deaf, just didn't
hear, wasn't listening. Then
a voice inside me erupted.
I heard everything
much more than I wanted.

WAITING

Sometimes, in a flurry
of feathered wings I see something
that isn't there. Not a bird
sitting and fluffing but a gauzy thing.
The brook at the edge of the woods
shimmers in a hint of white
but no angel appears.

COLOR HAPPENED

Bees vibrated with anticipation.
Rhododendron buds tight
little artichokes, tempered
by the sun, purple opened
to brilliant fuchsia, pretentious
and gaudy as green.

THE PURSUIT

I caught a glimpse of happiness
strange, unnerving but,
I knew what I was after.
The struggle, fierce relentless
tooth and claw, ethics justice
honesty, forgotten in that pursuit.
I don my shiny armor, heavy hot
my horse in hasty flight
breath against the wind across
the highlands into the woods. Deer
wait startled at my clamor. But
I am lost, forgotten too my mission.
What am I pursuing in this crazy flight?
Oh yes, I remember, happiness.

AGAIN

When truth unsettles
the mind's logic, tangles
calculated reason into lies
the burden knots the stomach
flips the heart and I say
for no reason, or logic,
please God.

OR OZ

On a Sunday, I woke up happy.
I mean happy. Thoughts of love
death, past future, forgotten
stones in the cemetery
irrelevant. I swear, I felt connected
or disconnected, like the seventh
state of being, or leaving Kansas.
Maybe I'm in heaven.

ON A SATURDAY

I got up crying. Birds circled
with laments, spirituals
learned in morning hymns
reverberating from stones
in God's houses. Enough!
Where are the jesters
in rainbow suits, white gloves
juggling colored balls.
Let the fun begin.

IMITATING

I could caw-caw like a crow
an easy sound, but a waxwing,
goldfinch, golden-crowned kinglet
or flicker, twist my tongue
not made for trilling.
I am content with caw-caw
the crow a fine bird, but I envy,
am in awe of fine-tuned notes
I cannot sing.

MEMORIES OF FLYING

I walked the night road
away from dark rooms
where my mother cried.
As a child I ran
leaped into the air high
above the ground
in that instant felt, I think,
a glimmer of happiness.

UNDERSTANDING

I haven't a clue
what went wrong. Birds
screeched vacated pines.
I thought it my right
like animals, not to suffer
but happiness is just luck,
dark times a matter
of chance, I'll never know
why, it just happened.

AND

Hey Josephine come on out and
play. I can't my brother is sick and,
hey Jose come on, come on out and
play, just a little while. I can't
my brother is sick and my mother,
and my mother, is dead. Oh! my mother,
and my mother is dead and she asked me,
she asked to get her a bowl of soup and
I didn't and so she died and now
and now, I can't go out to play.
I yelled down the stairs across the hall,
and I can't, and don't want to, and,
and can't come out to play!

OBSESSING

That mood again, feeling of gloom
not war, global warming, that magnitude.
A trivial thought obsesses
overwhelms, suffocates, clutches at me
like an unwelcome lover.
It is annoying, troublesome, unless
you cared, unless you loved me.
So, do you love me do you, please,
just a trivial thought I'll obsess
but do you, this is not trivial
I need to know, do you?

RIDDLES

A prophet spoke in riddles,
said, a white cow from a black
but a golden calf from neither,
danced for rain as a forest burned.
I am a rock with no understanding.
The prophet says, it is a sin to look
at King Tut's face. Strangers gazed,
he knew and suffered. If I could dance
I'd make rain, if I could swim, no longer
be a rock, if I knew the answers, I could
help King Tut to the next world.

FADED ROSES

When I was young, no flowers
colored the windowsills.
Wild ones, blue and yellow
grew in the fields
never thought to put them
in the bare gray house.
But roses bloomed, a bit faded
on the tattered tablecloth
under tinted glasses of tea.

WINTER SCENE

The crisp mountain air froze
the thin blue sky, under snow
bushes waited for sap to flow.
Two geese lingered late in
ice-bound brook, legs locked
frozen tight, their low-pitched
sound like the hunting hound,
yearned for flight, no words
for this sight, this plight,
night fright, this sight.

MUST BE AN ANGEL

Reflected in the pond
by the beaver's dam, a white
light slashed the cobalt sky,
the sun momentarily dazzling,
a vision appeared, an angel.
Definitely an angel,
came as I did to contemplate
the profoundly impressive,
definitely awesome, dam.

REVEALED

Something, feathered wings
revealed itself, shyly took shape.
Mist surrounded it, music,
as it fluttered down
where cattails grew.
I thought an angel, but
something else sat proudly,
waited to be recognized.

THIS WINTER

Cold depressing dangerous
and yes, I know, beautiful.
I could stay, survive but
wanted out, forget frozen
skies grey hills.
The deer stands, one leg up
on powdered snow, listens,
turns to the woods
disappears. I could too,
but it's not that easy.

BIRD SEED

Winter at my door birds
at the feeder. I say idiots,
why have you not fled
snow falls white, dead.
I say it, dead. A song
like a flute, a red cardinal
against snow, red.
I say it, red, red.

WORRYING

I worry about the world
turning, whirling in space.
I feel it, my stomach
sensitive to motion.
Men gathering to make war
makes me sick, my heart
sensitive to life, living.
I worry. Worrying makes me sick,
might even kill me and, I am
especially sensitive to dying.

CHAPTER 3
FAMILY HISTORY: Growing Old

TORTURE

If I were hung upside down
put on a bed of nails, water dunked
other tortures, fingernails pulled,
the hopeless deterioration
of old age, not as sadistic maybe,
but the concept is there.

THE BOOK

I looked up from the book
jolted from the civil war
withdrew from the scene
of carnage, battles, death.
Exhausted I acknowledged
defeat, too old for all this
dying, I slipped back to life
but only temporarily.

READING

I turned the last page.
Immersed in fantasy I twirled
around remembering
a passionate past, soared
as if I was young and fantastic
but it was too exhausting.

SIGNS

Signs are clear, unmistakable.
I look in the mirror horrified
time to think of options
driving the car into a tree
pills less painful not as reliable.
Just do it, give it up. Old age
relentless heartless, a bully
and I am a sniveling coward.

DINNER GUEST

It was an accident. The bottle
clinked the wine glass
knocked it over. A red stain
on white lace, amazing.
Startled, my hand shook.
Heirlooms, a break would've
spoiled dinner. I stared at
the red blossom all evening.
It was rather beautiful.

SEPTEMBER

The last warm days darken
old stars from the past still bright
apples fall from gnarled trees.
The sky older, so beautiful
I can hardly breathe.
An apple falls.

ADRIFT

My anchor detached, I am afloat
no shore mountain tree
no safety line, destination.
I drift unable to steer
hold the wheel of this hapless
vessel. Alone, I watch
as an ominous storm descends
and pulls me out to sea.

STEPPING OUT

I open the door cautiously.
Curled on the coach, my depression
whimpers clutching at me.
Under quilts in bed my body shivers
furious at my taking leave.
Work undone I stand uncertain
trying to get myself together
escape before the figure writing
at the table looks up grabs me.
I am a traitor yet heroic thinking
I can leave them all behind.

A LIKELY STORY

She fell, broke her arm, other things
couldn't move. Anyone out there?
She waited, flew to a place lush soft
and easy, a hammock swinging.
She pulled her legs up holding on
as best she could to feathered wings
that screeched like a siren.

SPRING

Green shoots push up earth
the world spins around
I feel no shift tilt sign of
movement. Yet spring silently
is pushing throbbing bursting.
I will miss it as I prepare
to spin away.

ATTACK

It sits waiting to pounce.
Humped, hissing lips drawn back
fangs set. My skin crawls
heart pounds I tremble in fear
panic, waiting for the inevitable.
The cat, old age, descends.
Futilely, I cover my head.

PREPARATION

In the mirror my face pulled
into whirlpools. One look enough
to age me, chair by the window
with the lace curtains prepared.
I laughed, lace curtains, I hated
lace curtains. But it wasn't funny.

THE GARDEN

Roses hung from bushes
lilacs rhododendrons
apple blossoms
sumptuous spontaneous
spring filled my eyes with tears.
I left the Garden of Eden
in Adam's hands.
A tragic event, one tulip.

COMPANY

I lie in bed curled up with self-pity
company enough.
I miss crab apples rotting
on the ground, green pines
stabbing the sky. Easy work
leaves me aching. I sit in the garden
with potted flowers
a bird sings, the weeds push up
dirt, a stone. Time passes
in its own good time.

ANOTHER WINTER

Still alone. I used to say I love it.
Now I am old know more about life
like that hermit dead
in a heap of trash, crazy
the way I will go.
Tired of news the whole damn world.
There are footsteps. Not expecting
anyone I keep my door locked.
Someone is knocking.

SCARY

A turtle-dove coos in the night.
I think a dove but don't know.
Young, I ran chasing wings
shiny things. Now
the heat dries geraniums
cooing repeats. My hand
on my knee like stained tea.
This is me, a fairy, scary.

THE FUNERAL

Flowers pink in a vase. No need
to waste them after the funeral.
She lay in bed, her side, the other
empty, stretched her hand
carefully. It lay there in empty space
a branch extended.
She closed her eyes, smiled.

LOSING IT

I wake up, still dark
the world in creation.
The windows brighten.
Next morning again. Now
I am certain day follows night
I can concentrate on gravity.
I worry. My brain wilting
a flower rusting curling into itself.
The door closes, the key thrown
into a well. I empty water all day
fill barrels buckets, the key not found.
What will I do with all this water.

THE BED

Life centered on the bed
open window, scent of lilacs
unbearable. Her body
not weighted to carve a form
but death, deeply impressed
next to her, fitful spasmodic
like an old lover or a rapist
cruel careless sweating
heavy, shaking her bones.
Somehow, not gracefully
she will endure all these bedfellows
pre-empting that malevolent place.

PEACHES

I buy peaches overripe
for cooking. My stomach
rebels at raw. Who was it,
said, 'I grow old, I grow old',
I shall wear my trousers rolled,
do I dare to eat a peach'?

PRIVACY

Old age is insufferable, she said.
Such indignity, unbearably offensive.
I can't submit to such humility.
Disgraceful contemptible
I would rather die!
I will not concede.
Privacy is still in my command!
Long live the queen.

NEW DIRECTIONS

Black Elk stands in the circle
centered. Lately he is hopeless
forlorn, weary of prophesies
warriors go East, buffalo West
the winter North.
No patience for directions
growing old he only wants
to head South.

DECISIONS

Let me be blunt before I lose
my mind. Serious. A friend's white
hair turned blue, she fell down
the stairs breaking something, went
to a home, met a ninety- year old
and bloomed. Think about it. I am
not making this up, remember,
brush teeth, keep wits about you
watch step and avoid at such
high prices, getting old.

THIS LIFE

OK, so this is my life.
The usual. Everyone knows
I have my secrets, fantasies fears
an urgent need for a miracle
a dramatic leap of faith. I know
it will never happen. I'm too old
and leaping is out of the question.

REVELATIONS

Some say they had
a revelation, spoke to God
bright light before death.
I wish I believed. Maybe
a miracle happened
and I unaware let it pass.
The only thing left is old age.
But you never know.

MORE SERIOUS

A red sky, red lake, a blue bird
sings a keen song but still
my spirit falls. A nightingale
swoops, catches it, flings it up.
I am so lucky.

NATURE

I sit outside contemplating
nature, sky trees flowers birds
all that moves, all that's still
endless fascination.
Yet, it is apparent that
everything moving or still
is not the least
interested in me.

HIM

I knew him, lived with, loved.
Time leaned heavily, turned
his lips blue drained pigment
from his hair suffered his hands
with cold. For me, time came
in seconds minutes hours
unfettered into days. His pulse
fading, what was I thinking as
the light left his eyes,
I could escape?

NEEDING WORDS

He whispers 'I am dying'.
My ear close, his breath
sucking at the air
pulling at words I long
to hear. His face stretched
trying, only a whisper
'I am', dying unfinished.

SUMMER MEMORY

I put more wood in the stove.
The house still cold.
I can't remember summer
heat, green landscapes
potted flowers. I forget names
places, sometimes pain, but
happiness I do recall, vaguely.

A POEM FOR NOW

The sky is blue. What is true
has always been true.
Things constant, green yellow
and red, assurance I'm not dead
but truth, not always told, lies
more comforting to the old.

TEN SPEEDS

She was skinny, bent
old, ridiculous black tights
a biker's jacket, helmet
ready for the finish,
really quite fantastic.
Why not the zippered leather
ten-speed bike to grace her
the race not over, superbly
dressed, slightly drugged,
she is still a contender.

THE SERMON

Two and two not always
four, she said. I knew
my addition was flawed.
All parts not the whole
she continued, and the meek
shall inherit the earth.
I didn't believe a word. Meek,
I inherited old dishes, my brother
the farm, acres of earth, but I
knew, flawed and old as I was
what that sermon meant.

THE JOURNAL

In a room viewing snow-bound
woods, a cup on a table
an open journal abandoned.
I have given up writing
the meaningless chronology
of my day, concluded, and I
may be wrong, that nobody
in their right mind wants to read
anything but war, cruelty killing
catastrophes and other
exciting stuff. And sports.

DESSERT

The woman met her new
husband in America. He surprised
her. His farm, a cabin, no running
water, wood against the back wall
he made a fire while she sat
on the bed. It occurred to her
she didn't know this man
had no place to run.

THANKFUL

Good wishes make me bristle.
I can't be thankful. I'm desperate
for the youth I squandered
unknowingly, stupidly. I want
to run leap ride a bike. I'm glad
there are no bombs falling
but it doesn't help. Old is old
tired, afraid and still stupid.

ANYPLACE

I'm tired of being tired
want to run, jump race fly
with the birds beat the drum
dance the circle of fire.
If I could run that mile
on sand, rocky fields, woods
even hot coals, anyplace
at all will do, if I could only run.

AWAKENINGS

The first robin is not
a thing of beauty but
a chilled bird, clumsy
and fretful. I am old, keen
for the first signs of spring
not expecting much
from awakenings
metamorphosis is painful,
I suspect, urgent, uncertain.
Here I am, a cold nervous
bird, longing for life.

END GAME

It is really sad, well,
more than sad,
it is devastating
to give up on love.

JUST WONDERING

Will you miss me
when I'm gone. I tremble
when I think, all the things
I will never see, hear feel
touch. Nothing.
Most of all I wonder
if I will miss you.

CHAPTER 4
TALKING TO THE PROPHET

THE CAVE

The prophet stumbles out
makes his prediction
gropes back to the cave.
How he survives is uncertain.
Gaunt, and like me believes
the world is coming to an end,
not a staggering prophesy
life drags on in that direction.
He feels a failure, never witnessed
his prophesies but I am certain
that very soon God will
make an honest man of him.

REPENT

The prophet rode a mule.
Both old bony barely alive.
Still he preached 'Repent!'
tore at his chest. In a moment
of great magnitude the mule
was inspired to speak.
This profound truth
was clearly heard but
the prophet shocked, denied it.
I heard and denied it too.

THE CIRCLE

In a distant land the Sphinx sits.
The moon in the East smiles
the red sun squeezes
between two megaliths.
A prophet, inspired by the circle
of stones moves a mountain.
The Sphinx not to be outdone
sings a triennial song, the prophet
with shameful abandonment
dances with the Goddesses.

PREDICTION

The bird whistled, the prophet
woke up saw the light and said,
this is the last day.
Always grouchy I ignored him
pulled grapes from vines
watered the spotted cows.
The sun dropped, the moon rose
the prophet unabashed yet
alarmed at this unbecoming situation
turned to blame Me
but I, compassionate
offered the pulled grapes.

MEMORY

My father milking cows
the smell of the barn
no prophet to predict
when this memory would end.
It permeated every rocky field
God ran across
with His red banner. I am
no prophet but willing
to predict that memory
will persist even in eternity.

SOUNDS

The prophet listens
to the electric sounds,
the moon rising, sap flowing
apples growing. He is keen
on the hum of the stars
the whiz as planets whirl by
the cries of the earth
as its heart breaks.

QUESTIONS

We don't know who we are
what we are here for came
from, going. We know basics
how to kill plunder violate.
What else? I ask the prophet.
He talks in riddles
the fluctuating space between
Mars Jupiter and God.
His answers incomprehensible
so, we are stuck on basics.

QUICKSAND

A prophet came out of the woods
said not to go there is quicksand.
Some listened others
went in did not come out.
My father also a prophet
said it was safe. I do not know
who is right or if it matters.
I am afraid of the woods
and prophets scare me.

A NORMAL DAY

Flowers were dying, I watered them.
The yellow bus stopped, children
ran out a dog barked.
The prophet appeared and said
the world will come to an end.
Flowers perked up, the prophet
rearranged his words,
in the end the world will come.
I did not understand the new
arrangement so I picked flowers
pulled the shades in the house
and invited the prophet in.

MORE QUESTIONS

I asked him, he didn't know.
How could that be, he is a prophet.
He said he answers the right
questions. It didn't matter.
I was heart-broken.
Who will I turn to. I lost faith.
The prophet told me
the right question was the answer.
I didn't believe him or his riddles.
And I am still heartbroken.

GOOD EATING

John my friend, remembers food
he ate thousands of years ago.
He loves good food, did not believe
Eve was tempted by an apple. I agreed.
He was astounded that a book was written
on that food choice and the indelible
effect it had on world's consciousness.
The prophet wasn't interested but
did consider feasting on roast lamb.
John's favorite was pickled pig's feet
though anything pig was out.
John would not have survived
forty years of manna but
the sacrificial bar-b-ques satisfied
his yearning for filet. I am trying
to tempt him, the prophet suggested
baked apples, not in jest, as prophets
are seldom funny so I vehemently
opposed. We settled on Chinese.

THE TEST

The prophet's test was a few short
answers. Choose carefully he said.
Is it 'The best of times or the worst
of times.' It is urgent to know.
If it is the best of times we are lost
if it is the worst of times
there is still hope. It is confusing.
I know I will fail.

WONDERING

I know from Henry James
that there is an element of dull
rage in my consciousness.
It keeps me wondering if it is
helplessness or hopelessness
that simmers there. The prophet,
wisdom always ready says
it's a waste to ponder what
is on Henry James' mind.
It will evaporate with
the smell of coffee.

TRUE STORIES

It was creepy. The people
were ordinary yet they did
things unimaginable, murder
torture worse, without thinking
like an every-day kind of thing
not a pang or shiver, like walking
from the zoo eating ice-cream.
The prophet says he knows
what I am thinking, that maybe
I could do that too. Could I?

COUNTING ON SUCCESS

Swarms of people, ants, bees
fleas, lice roaches, mosquitoes.
Soldiers, tanks armored trucks
planes bombs bullets blasts.
The prophet reminds me
not to forget surgery,
arms legs skulls, faces eyes
brains guts genitals, hearts.
I am despondent but he
sees success, in one tulip.

SURVIVAL

The prophet is partial
to the beauty of winter
the brilliance of sun on snow
dark pines, red cardinals
stunning the white. A lone
deer in a field of silence.
The prophet says we are far
from the war, all is well.
Beauty is fragile, winter long
the prophet not a wiz at math
cannot calculate distance.

THE PROPHET

The first time I saw the prophet
sitting on a rock in the woods
eating berries, he offered me some.
A spotted fawn at his feet, red
cardinals preened on branches
I hardly noticed, consumed with grief.
I asked him, he said there is no secret
remember the good times
and bring a pot for the berries.

HOW DID I KNOW

He was a prophet, he told me
sitting on a rock, eating apples.
I didn't believe him, I longed for answers
to my malignant grief. He stroked his
beard, his eyes in the tree tops.
I followed his gaze to the light
shimmering there. I ate an apple
as I contemplated his answer.

THE SNAKE

The prophet blasted a whistle
on a blade of grass, the boys pleaded
more, but a movement in the grass
a snake swallowing a frog.
The boys jumped, frightened
at the frog's violent struggle,
ran, returned with a knife.
The world is a snake, devours us all,
said the prophet. The snake takes a life
the frog still alive, you take two.
The boys, focused on this grisly sight
and being a true story, missed
a prophetic lesson in philosophy.

THE HINT

I sat with the prophet, told him
my grief. He says, let the lamb
feed for a week before you take it
from its mother. Very compassionate
but does not help me. He tells me
to go home, think about the mother.
I do. It has made my grief deeper.

THE PINE

Meet me at the rock
near the pine where the prophet
waits. You know, we've been
there. Pervaded at dawn by fairies
mysterious creatures, things
that fly flicking light, fur and wings
all sorts of trilling filling sounds
at the rock near the pine
where we meet sometimes
even when we're not there.

CHAPTER 5

TALKING TO MYSELF: THE COMING OF THE MESSIAH

ONE

I want to witness a miracle.
Not the everyday kind but
the coming of the Messiah
shining like a rock-star in sequins.
Actually, I want to see if what
the Rabbi says, will happen.
What does he say? It is too
ridiculous, preposterous. But
better than Elvis. I could
follow Him wherever,
however, raising the dead,
(right before my eyes?)
I don't think so.

TWO

I'll be ready to greet Him
when He comes. I say 'Him',
who in Her right mind
would take such a position.
Anything could happen
stoning burning rape
any number of horrors. So
the Messiah will be a man,
God help him.

THREE

I'll roast a lamb, unblemished
invite everyone to meet Him
mark the sign on my door
as it is inscribed. You think I am
presumptuous, crazy, you are
skeptical, lack faith. Laugh
but I know the truth, the truth!
As sure as the sun rises, sets
the Messiah will sit at my table
and eat like any ordinary man.

FOUR

I am worried. This unknown Man
this Messiah, what will happen
when He comes. I'm used to things
coping, afraid of change.
A Woman maybe, take us
on a picnic eat hard-boiled eggs
build sand castles, fairytales
of a pearly ruby world, everyone
lives happily ever after, even longer.
But Him?

FIVE

Will my profound questions
mysteries of good and evil
be answered, a huge universal
'A-ha!' or no answers. The world
transformed, I will no longer
remember the questions or
if it mattered.

SIX

There are propositions but first
a party. A potluck. Mrs. L. brought
a roast Mrs. R. pudding, the table
heavy, the odor pleasing.
The Messiah ate heartily
performed a few miracles
some healings but no answers.
Then, in a blinding blaze of light
He ascended to the sky.
Mrs. E. called 'come back
you forgot to taste my honey cake!'

SEVEN

Nothing I'd like better 'love
thy neighbor.' I have a neighbor
with four dogs. God help me
I need some sleep. If the Messiah
saves only the righteous
maybe there's hope.

EIGHT

I took Him to bless a wedding.
The dance began, women
one side, men the other.
Lifted high He sat above us
beaming. The men circled
hypnotic, I mesmerized, joined.
Frantic they waved me away.
The music stopped the Messiah
eased to the floor, approached me.
I trembled. He was something.
Better than a rock- star.

NINE

Why a Messiah? This
a distressing question.
We are alone in the universe
need help desperately. A hero
some kind of superman
fairy Godmother, an alien.
I don't care much, any Messiah
will do even a homeless musician
with a mission.

TEN

It is unlikely, a wish hardens
into shape and there He is
the Messiah. However,
what do I know, really know,
nothing. I will live I will die
and if the Messiah comes
as the Rabbi says, and raises
the dead I will know everything
of both worlds, ultimate secrets
and then I will believe.
The Rabbi will be so happy.

ELEVEN

Ocean floors will lock, desserts
bloom, rain forests lush-up
plundered wounded earth
heal, when the Messiah comes.
If the Rabbi is mistaken, after all
a poor man with nine children
the earth will still rage. The Rabbi,
despite children, is a scholar. If he
says he is sure, he is sure.

TWELVE

I will ask the Messiah about
Ravensbruck, that select
concentration camp for women.
God help us. The Messiah is quiet.
Who knows what he thinks.
Why did it happen? We are entitled
to know at least that when the
Messiah comes. But, He won't tell
even if He knows.

THIRTEEN

He will shine, a reflective light
about Him, sequins like
the King, when He comes.
How else would we know?
Suddenly, fear doubt disbelief
vanish, even suffering.
It is unlikely, but who knows.
It will be a huge relief
to finally be happy.

CHAPTER 6
INCANTATIONS: Old-Wives Tales

1.

It happened in the barn, cat
jumped horse, crazy it held fast.
Chickens refused to lay eggs, cows
no milk. Spirits possessed them.
Trouble. Hang a blanket bang
milk pail, if the blanket shakes
spirit left cow entered horse.
It wings to the sky with other
horsemen. War violence death
chickens, cows, life is uncertain.
Now is the hour. Watch out.
FATHER save us!

2.

They gave her room, spit
passing her house
covered the baby, mumbled
a blessing. She was possessed
cursed, maybe a witch
or a saint prophet healer if
only they knew.
Poverty sickness death
power greater from the grave.
Look to heaven, knock on wood.
Don't talk, think, what you say
may be possessed of the truth.
The truth!
Father save us!

3.

A witch they said. Patriarchs
examined her never exposed
body, private flesh, curved
white mottled too. In the dark
of her armpit a blemish
a witch's mark, certain as hell.
The burning took time, crackled
sparked smoked. They watched.
The odor neither pleasing nor troubling
as half, no more than half, the women
in town drifted into the sky.
MOTHER save us!

4.

Bats at the windows, thief at the door
drought and dust, keep your eyes down.
The house is on fire, Knock on wood,
run fast. Father, save us.

5.

The woman covered in black
eyes peering behind a net,
an evil temptress. Protect us
from her, her from us,
from him, him from her. A knife
under that black, just in case.
MOTHER save us!

6.

The moon followed
when I walked. One night
it stopped. The prophet said
when the moon refused
to walk across the sky
the earth shifted, trees
and boulders changed
wolves howled. Praying,
mystic charms no longer
worked. MOTHER.

7.

Knowing the past
the futility of the present
I can't help project
into that unchartered
imaginary time, an awful
inevitable future.
FATHER Help.

8.

Lord Father Mother Ghosts
Prophets Saints Angels
Him Her It.
Is anyone there?

THE DECISION

Please dear God
is anyone listening.
I pray anyway. A bang
the door opens rush of cold air
God enters. Michelangelo's God.
I say, come in get warmed up
I offer hot soup, no answer.
God yawns goes to sleep.
I think He sleeps too much
most of last century. I try to
get His attention. My violin
is out of tune. God yawns.
I take out the gun, point it
at Him then turn it on myself.
I have God's attention.
But who to aim at.

CHAPTER 7
MOMENTS IN STONE

FORGIVING

I forgave my mother
for dying, my father too
but not my brother. When
he left I ran into the woods
my bleeding- heart dripping.
The old house waited. There
I could hang by bruised heart
on a hook to heal.

THEY SAY

Dead is dead, that's it.
There is evidence some
have returned from disasters
falling off the mountain
drowning in the sea
tidal waves, epidemics.
I get on with life, still,
he stands there, dead
to be sure, but who knows,
it may not last long.

A DEATH IN THE FAMILY

Lightning strikes, death,
like an arm a leg cut off
dismembers, life goes on
the rock rolls up rolls down
senseless. How do I cope.
I have not learned yet.
I am still dealing with
the rock.

THE MINIMAL OF MEANING

Perpetual silence.
Birth death grief
awe flowers disbelief
music God, despair.
Breathe in, out,
sun air burial,
a handful of dirt,
the pickax.

RITUALS OF GRIEF

I am a refugee, lost
in a forbidding land, death
that unfamiliar territory
a map of lost treasures.
It is a bitter hardship
but, with studied care
I learn the tedious rituals.

SOME KIND OF COLOR

A shaft of sunlight on my bed
intrudes. Flowers drink water
the color of pain. I am not
in the mood for bright.
Grief, gray swamp brown
musty green, some kind of
yellow, I know it, smell,
feel, it oozes out a bit
bleeds into the bedcovers.

WHEN TO DIE

She died in winter
not meaning to.
The ground frozen. She
was buried anyway.
People huddled in icy wind
wanting to go home. They did.
What were they thinking
leaving her there
freezing. Frozen.

WHEN TO BE BURIED

If she waited for spring
to die, could they bury her
when flowers bloomed
pink, sweet scented
alive with honey bees
the earth soft muddy
filled with water,
maybe better in winter.

SIGHTINGS

When sighting birds
dressed in black, I think
of dying, an ordinary thought.
I am anchored, welded
here, a tree, mountain,
my spirit raging, a volcano
moving, equal in effort maybe,
to the flight of a bird.

A SHORT VISIT

He is here, visiting
floating in on clouds.
He says he has work, he must go.
His ax soundless, a tree falls,
his hammer taps, leaving no mark.
He visits in the mourning room
no one notes his presence.
He leaves as he came
through the window.
He has work to do,
somewhere.

PAST-LIFE

A memory, he is fitting stones
together, shapes coming alive,
bones sharp to the touch.
His ghost hovers just
out of reach. I call his name,
a familiar sound, ending
in silence. There he is
alive no doubt
but still transparent.

MINDFULNESS

Be mindful, alert
to the snake, its bite
the tree its fruit
names carved there
forgotten. In the garden,
when one is off-guard
death strikes unmindful
of promises, and
those left behind.

WATCHING THE MOUNTAIN

On a day like any other
I knew who was taken
was never coming back.
Stars kissed me, waves rocked
me like a velvet baby, moon
walked at my side, sky
hid heaven, dark as an eclipse.
That day started as a lullaby
but one person removed
moved a mountain over me.

JUST BEFORE SPRING

After my mother, my father
died. My brother and I
ran, a pasture now a forest
chased the wind, poked
the moon, the sun cold as ice.
My father called.

SO MUCH FOR LIFE

How could I know
at ten, running, jumping
a faun bright as the night,
it would be like this. Life,
traitor to promised things.

THAT PLACE

Where is that somewhere
life goes on, blackbirds
on a pine, red birds
color a birch, speckled fish
spawn in cattails, a face
reflected in rusty water
trimmed in air.

SKIING

Spring quietly bloomed
in the cemetery, stones
on stones, half the village,
my brother too. I brought
roses, talked easily now what
should have been said
before, when he looked
radiant, tanned, like he just
flew off the ski slope.
Before roses.

WHAT WILL I DO

When the moon disentangles
from the trees and shoots
up the sky in full glory
will I witness alone
that glorious event
or have you orchestrated
with your artful pranks,
pulled that splendid blue
velvet curtain from that side
dazzling me again.

SIGNS

The sky gave no sign,
the shape of a cloud, a butterfly.
Knowing if I sat here forever
on his grave, a lifetime
it will not happen.
But after? Who knows,
maybe then.

WAITING

Even if the sky falls,
the earth splits,
I would wait.
When I walk head down
watching for obstacles
stones, ghosts in the way
I put out my hand.

TURNING AWAY

Living in the visible world
no longer pleases me.
Catastrophes come and go,
war, earthquakes, the deceit
of a friend. The grave.
In disbelief I turn away. But,
the color of the sky is stunning,
green as the grass.

TIME

Time marches this New Year
not to drums, snappy
uniforms, bright buttons
but names, his he him. Why,
how could it be.
He is gone. Time stopped.
No drum beats, shiny buttons
this Year, I march alone
in a dark shirt, clearly ripped.

THE LAST WILL

My brother sat in the dark
his hands on his knees.
It was so gloomy I hated it
wanted to run get away
scared, tired of people dying.
God, I wished it was over.
But the chair my brother sat in
was immensely empty.
Oh! My God!

LILIES

I never saw someone dead
so, I kept my distance.
She paid no heed to flowers
cared not for pity, grief.
She, already comfortable
somewhere else. I looked
with childish eyes wondering
what did death have to do
with me. If I stayed my distance
I'd never catch it.

GAMES

We jumped rocks catching
branches swinging to the ground.
We showed-off, moving stars
spinning the sun directing
the brook's flow.
He grew tall, secrets
became stones of a different kind.
He rose above
the great flapping geese
leaving the game behind.

THE BALL

The baseball field,
a dirt road to the barn
now woods, young saplings
cover first base, a birch
marks second. He hit the ball
clear over the barn. The game
fell apart, death stole a run
slipped home.

THINGS I MISS

Geraniums in the window.
I don't remember if I missed
my mother. My father
stays with me, refuses to let go,
my sister and brothers too.
The full moon on the dark
road attends me on the way
home. How could I forget
the house is empty.

FORGETTING GRIEF

Watching TV, something funny
furiously futilely funny. I laughed
and laughed, it felt so good.
Life was funny, so painfully
funny. I laughed, forgetting
for a minute, completely
forgetting, that he was dead.

CHAPTER 8
WAR

DIFFERENCES

Winter wind freezes the walls
of the house to the ground.
Snow drifts high. I drink tea
listen to world news, wars floods
evil men in power. They talk
of irreconcilable differences.
My heart freezes.
What does irreconcilable mean?

THEY KNEW

We don't need prophets
to tell us the world is dying.
The Peace-keepers on corners
black signs left in trash
one flood washes another it's
all the same. My life is almost
over, why should I care. I go
home watch the game but
I'm in a nasty mood.

WEATHER

Going outside was painful.
Cold penetrated artificial
fibers, even fur. Pure misery.
The prophet canceled the war
just too cold. But the general,
in sheepskin, declared it warm.
Sheep were slaughtered
despite bleating and hailstone
the war went on.

STATIONS

I knew nothing about the train
when it pulled into the station.
A child hung out the window
screaming. Where the iron track
went I learned, was unimaginable
and even worse it was true.

THE TRACK

The children waved. The train shrieked
clickety-clack, black smoke shrouded
those standing on the platform
men with guns made a mess of life.
In the country birds sang
as they did in disasters.

HUNTERS

The hunters gathered, guns slung
low. Animals ran, not the prey
but hung from trees, drained blood.
The echo of the train led to
the iron tracks. I knew nothing
of what was or what was to be.

LIFE GOES ON

Anger deep rooted, poisoned.
It's done, I said, coiled my hair
swept the kitchen, listened
to the news. Soldiers marched
prepared for war. I tied my hair
while the tanks rolled, drank tea
as a million refugees crossed
a border. I baked a cake
while Rome burned.

HAVING LUNCH

I can go out for lunch
sandwich, pizza, knowing
I can go again tomorrow. I guess
the people in Baghdad thought
the same, in Warsaw they
gave up the idea. In Vietnam
as far as I know, they never
went out for lunch.

WINTER BIRD

In the middle of the winter
a bird on my window sang,
beak wide. I understood,
fearfully eyed the world,
past, middle, every side
of the incoming rising tide,
terrified.

DARK NIGHT

Why men were on horseback
I am not certain.
I glimpsed a face reflected
from the light of a distant star,
a glint of steel, a handle
took shape, barrel of a gun.
The horses, no constellation
had a destiny far from heavenly.

BELLS

Bells sounded another war.
Nobody knew what to do.
Some foolishly turned to Darwin
others to Einstein, a matter
of relativity. Most remained
with God preferring a Deity.
Despite these three, evil
reigned, the earth quivered
some survived, returned
to the garden, others
to the apes but most were
sucked into the black hole.

THE BOOK

The boy looked up, the man
in fancy uniform
took the handle of his gun
slammed it into boy's head
he fell to the ground
blood gushed from his nose.
I read this in a book.
I'll never open it again
don't trust the author to say
such unbelievable things.

UNFIT MOTHER

It was the war
when all the men left
and never returned.
I thought I taught my sons well
how to use a spoon say please
and thank you
useless words in war.
How could I have been
such an unfit mother.

FRIENDS AND ENEMIES

One man died accidentally
thirty-three died in ambush
eighty by hand grenade
six hundred taking a hill
half losing it twenty in morning
raid nine hundred going
into a forest seven hundred
going out ninety-nine one sunny
week a hundred more a rainy one
sixty-three carelessly.
That was the sum total,
the enemy count not precise
before the war ended.

INVASION

Which war was it
the one with bow arrows
swords or guns. I ran
into the woods watched
as they killed the chickens
pigs, rode off with them and
my horse leaving dust.
The cat under the porch alive
and the men, with some streak
of humanity, left the water
in the well untouched.

MEMORIAL

In the season of winter
frozen trees held up
clouds breaking the flight
of smoke falling on snow
in dirty film of ashes.
Wood ashes, not human,
from innocent chimneys.
Trees bloomed with joy
clouds wept with happiness
and the sky opened
in abundant blue, savoring
the odor of wood ashes.

CONTINUED

More sacrifices, flesh burned
whole cities, a Holocaust.
The sky black with acrid smoke
ashes fell into tea cups
settled on trees in bloom
covered fields of violets
blew away to forests
mountain tops,
children inhaled.

TIMES OF NEED

I am here by the brook.
The fat vile geese honk
I own them. My stamp
on the sky, name carved
on every tree. Somewhere,
mountains move, populations
shift borders wired walled
guarded, every piece of land
a prison. Bad-tempered
creatures follow me, slop
the road. In this nasty world
it is significantly important
to own geese, fat vile and
succulent, in times of need.

FORGIVE

Life should ask for forgiveness
for what it did.
Traumas catastrophes war.
I cling to any memory
of joy, hang on when evil
happens, like eating candy
and watching a horror movie.
I can't get up walk out
have to see how it ends.

ENCHANTED

Everywhere is fear.
Gods making demands,
killing thoughtless and easy.
Beware chants, the rattles
of sabers, madmen all.
This enchanted world
no longer magical.
GODMOTHER!

GIVING UP

Armies march, the earth
trembles explosions light
the sky. Men violate
women bleed children
die suffering.
God retreats
into a well of darkness
where he sits and shivers.

THE RETREAT

Napoleon sat in soft mink, all of Russia's wildlife wrapped around him. Ermine from the Ural Mountains caped his shoulders, silver fox around his neck its long baby face hanging on his chest, luxurious Siberian wolf capped his balding head and from the Northlands, musk deer and long-haired black bear tucked around his feet.

The Army
His army lay behind him stretched across the frozen tundra. Horses dead standing up, boy soldiers leaning like monuments against their sides. Napoleon rode out of Russia's winter leaving his army dazzling and frozen until Spring. It was a clean army he left behind, no dirty vulgar signs of life. No blood trickled from frozen veins into cancerous wounds, no cannons fired, no guns shot, no heavy artillery broke the silence of the snow.

CHAPTER 9
FAMILY HISTORY: The Child

STUCK

Time swung, a pendulum
past to present
neither here nor there
everywhere, a snowstorm
in spring. The mother died.
Jolted, the pendulum stuck.
The mother remained in the
past, the child too. Then
inevitably, time moved on.

SAYING GOODBYE

I am older
than my mother when she left
in a gray coat. Her bed
empty. Did she say goodbye.
Something more than words
left me A to Z to craft a memory
or define abandonment.
She will be forever younger
as I grow each year
closer to that far apart.

NOT HOW IT WAS

The words of that old song
'Oh, your daddy's rich, and
your mama's good looking'
wasn't like that at all.
Papa wasn't rich and mama
didn't care about good looking.
Once she wore red lipstick
and a black dress before she died.
Songs with words like 'hush,
don't you cry', not how it was
not a bit.

IF ONLY

She had talked
I would remember her.
Wisp of hair touch of hand
faded photo not nearly enough
to define a mother
but a voice, a word
could, if only she had talked,
have saved me.

NOT MY FAULT

Things went wrong. A round rock
chiseled flat with words
to scare the wolves, the child
not having mastered the alphabet
can hardly read 'Beloved' in stone.
Guilt, that nasty bird
squawks loudly.

THE THREE R'S

Only three words needed
to fracture a soul 'Rest in Peace'.
Words in Latin meaningless to
my mother who gagged
on sweet carrots. When A to Z
was revealed to me, words
beyond my age, I choked
on all that knowledge.

DISCOMBOBULATED

Sitting on a bench
feeding pigeons, that word
mysterious and indigestible as death
meaningless to her, the pigeons
who wobbled unsteadily cooed
as she sat crying, discombobulated.

RECALL

Memory trapped
the smell of the barn, spring
blossoms papa's voice a dark house
fear. I ran the field, rocks, woods
a bird screeched from a bush
a deer pounded and I ran
ran much too fast to stop.

WINTER COAT

The green coat, bought me before
she died, long heavy
shut out more than the cold
on that cemetery day.
Wrapped firmly below the knees
velvet hood hiding my face
unable to grasp betrayal
a consuming fear.

CHALLENGES

I jumped from stone to tree
swung to the ground
met every rocky challenge
but at home, timid afraid,
disturbing noises, things,
challenges too far to jump.

THE TRUTH ABOUT CHILDHOOD

I did not think adults cried.
Don't remember if I did
that cemetery day when cries
rent the air, primitive sounds
when language ceased, raw
grief clashed with disbelief.

ABOUT CHILDHOOD

Not a day I want to remember
or forget, the last time
I saw my mother. Memories
lean heavily on truths
fabricated from hearsay
told in secret bent out of shape.
A family broken and scarred.
How it clings to me.
Enough already.

WHITE LILACS

Pink azaleas on the table
near the sickbed. Take them out
she said, close the window, bird-song
no longer finds a nesting place here.
Remove any sign of life
that shakes a finger at me.

BURNING SUPPER

The food burnt, the pot
too. Papa yelled, stupid
I scraped the black pot
his voice in the din. I ran
to the woods, the smell
followed, held to my clothes
the scent of pines a sharp
reminder I had to go back.

HIS VOICE

My father's voice called
at night from the stairs
after he died. Jolted, I jumped up
answered him. No bolt of lightning,
I sat still every nerve edged
accusing me. At night
when dreams failed, I waited
in silence, permeated
with fear and anticipation
to hear his voice again.

HANGING ON

The flowers are dead.
A few leaves hang on. I miss
the color, other things I don't
remember, like my mother.
But my father stays. He resists
letting go. Just hangs on.

MEN'S TALK

When men talked
the child made-believe she heard
birds. Afraid of the hand lifted
the touch, she listened behind a stone
of silence, making believe.

WHITE SHEETS

We sat with bread and tea
as the white sheets flapped outside.
My mother, her flowered dress
faded daisies in a field of clover,
watched the sky. Hail like bullets
rat-tat-tat the sheets came down
over her, a giant caterpillar
covered like summer snow
almost like the day she died.

SITTING AROUND

Thick honey on black bread, ants
on sticky counters. Nobody dressed
for dinner like in books.
Good clothes were for funerals.
Aunt Min wore a dress.
Papa never noticed my shoes
too tight. We listened to news
nothing to do with life
except the weather.

OPEN HEART

Surgeons I know dug deep
the surgery ongoing almost daily
wounds a throbbing mess. Yes,
I will survive but my heart
stitched tight, skillfully
closed me up forever.

THE DAYS NEWS

Children waved goodbye.
The train shrieked away in black
smoke clickety-clack.
No headlines of those who stood
on the platform.
In the country birds sang
as they did in disasters.

A TOUCH

He called me crybaby.
He was right. My eyes pink
red around the blue
puckered shrunken. I cry, always
ready at a word, thought feeling,
or touch. Oh, a touch can set me off.
But it doesn't happen often.

CHAPTER 10
FAMILY HISTORY: Growing Old

GREEDY

As a child, I climbed
the tallest pine, touched
the sky, grabbed the stars.
I'm not a greedy person, but
having a few stars gave me
a solid footing in life.

WEATHER WATCH

Silence in the wind, it comes
and goes from oak to birch
sometimes moans,
birds flap away. I can tell
by the sky it will rain and
the wind shows signs of dying.
I don't take it personally.

STORM

Thunder and lightning wake
the night, flashing glints of lake
photo-shooting white, making
a fuss with green, cracking the sky
mean shots stop the storm.
Dawn staggers in, thin, gray
and exhausted.

SHIFTING

I cling with bare hands
to the rocks as the earth moves
an inch to make room for this,
old age. It is so unpredictable. Oh!
it is moving again.

ASLEEP

I never used to fall asleep
sitting up. I am not pained,
confused or despaired, just
any ordinary conversation,
the clink of teacups and I could,
on a straight, hard wood chair
without shame or memory
fall asleep sitting up.

DREAM

Once I dreamed I was old
watching TV, bored to death with life,
I would fall asleep sitting up. Bad habit,
aches and pains develop
where none existed. A word of caution,
if you dream of being old, and
it's not a dream, have a soft
cushioned chair in the kitchen
when women are talking of aging.

TOMORROW

I'm sick and afraid
I will die. Should I call someone
or just wait and see. I'll wait.
Maybe I'll feel better.
It's not the first time.
Doesn't help to worry, but
it's something to do until tomorrow.
But, what if, I better call.

THE WOLF

Waiting to pounce, latches on
each word I write, slobbers,
erasing quickly as it appears.
The race is frantic. I think blood
will run as the fight gets fierce,
intimate, I hear a satisfied
howling. The moon must be out.
See, I still know the moon,
the wolf, and I suspect,
the howling is mine.

SWEETS

Words like desolation and ice
make me feel old. I eat muffins,
chocolate melted in the sun
eases my mood. I smell spiced
ginger, there is Proust reading
aloud. I remember songs
I used to dance to. My chin
on my chest, I fall asleep
sitting up, Proust reading.

YELLOW

The color purple hurts
my eyes, red and pink,
disturbing, yellow much
too cheerful now, my heart
careful now, memories
of violets. I hate this, when
yellow is too bright
and red, unnerving.

NAMES

Everything has a name, a rose
is a rose. Planets, fish, the sea,
stars, daisies, pods of peas,
pennies dimes, tigers
and tea. The wonder and awe
all I see, lost in the name,
the mystery.

PLANTS

I have a plant, blossoms
once a year in winter, tip
of each leaf, red drop,
a pin-prick of blood. If
you watched forever, never
would see how this magic
happens, extraordinary,
immensely satisfying
if only once a year.

AFTER

Life is swift, short, final.
A bit of happiness, suffering
surprises, questions, mysteries.
Is there life after death?
Do I really want to know.

BREAKFAST

I know nothing of breakfast
buffets, sunlit patios, gardens
morning tea. Sniffing dogs,
wrought iron chairs
plump flowered cushions.
I have read in novels, romance
and murder, often wondered
how it must be to have
breakfast in crystal and silver,
but if one is old, a mug in a warm
kitchen surpasses settings
for romance and murder.

WHITE OUT

Forget driving, walking too.
Stay in the house, watch
winter. Was it meant for
old people to live here. Early,
we had fire, survived, evolved
to shovels. I am one of Darwin's
fittest, surviving when
the power goes out.

IMAGINE THAT

Life is not suited for everyone.
I believe that. I try to fit,
even manage cautiously
to glide along for the ride,
sometimes terrified. However,
there are monkeys swinging,
frogs sleeping in mud
leaches sucking blood.
Life suits them just fine.

THE QUESTION

So, how old are you, he insisted.
Oh, about a thousand million years.
No, you're not, you're a hundred zillion.
OK, I'm five. He laughed. No, I'm five!
Well, the mirror tells me one thing
my heart another, my legs offer
an opinion. I don't like it.
Something important was lost
between five and this. I intend to
make it up with this child or,
in the next life, even if it takes
a hundred zillion years.

www.ingramcontent.com/pod-product-compliance
Lightning Source LLC
LaVergne TN
LVHW012100070526
838200LV00074BA/3825